I am a New Creation

Written and illustrated by
SABRINA ADEWUMI

Thank you for purchasing an authorized copy of this book and for complying with copyright laws by not reproducing in any form without permission.
Copyright © 2023 All Rights Reserved

Scripture quotations marked NLT are taken from the Holy Bible, New Living Translation, copyright © 1996, 2004, 2015 by Tyndale House Foundation. Used by permission of Tyndale House Publishers, Inc., Carol Stream, Illinois 60188. All rights reserved.

For our three little birds,

and children everywhere, may you continue to

transform into the very best version of you!

Have you ever seen a caterpillar transform before your eyes?

It's amazing that those **squiggly** worms

Become *beautiful* butterflies!

When I think about that transformation,
so wonderfully designed -

The caterpillar changes into a whole

new

creature

It really blows my mind!

Then I remember what the Bible says:

(And I know what the Bible says is true)

In Christ we are a new creation; In Him all things are made new!

2 CORINTHIANS 5:17

Jesus died upon a cross

to set us free from sin

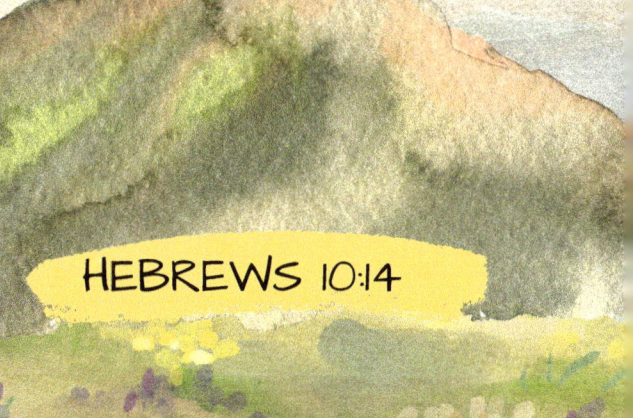

HEBREWS 10:14

That's why I opened up my heart

His promise was
new life in Him

My past has been wiped away!

As I walk with Him
　　　and grow in Him...

I'm being **transformed** every day!

Sometimes...
it's not so easy to change

But God helps me when I

pray

The caterpillar struggles for a while too

...until a butterfly emerges and flies away

In Christ I am a new creation

Becoming who He wants me to be

growing and maturing into the

very best version of me!

Someday I'll be a **whole new person**

This means that anyone who belongs to Christ has become a new person. The old life is gone; a new life has begun!

2 CORINTHIANS 5:17 (NLT)

www.ingramcontent.com/pod-product-compliance
Lightning Source LLC
Chambersburg PA
CBHW051402110526
44592CB00023B/2923